D1339856

AQIQA AND THE CROCUS and Other Stories

by
Hassina Khan

The Almond Press · 1983

Aqiqa and the Crocus and Other Stories
by Hassina Khan

With full page illustrations
by John Gilbert

Book design
by David Gunn

Copyright © 1983 The Almond Press

British Library Cataloguing in Publication Data:

Khan, Hassina
Aqiqa and the crocus.
I. Title
823'.914[J]   P27

ISBN 0-907459-22-6

Published by
The Almond Press
P.O. Box 208
Sheffield S10 5DW
England

Printed in Great Britain by
Dotesios (Printers) Ltd.
Bradford-on-Avon, Wiltshire
1983

CONTENTS

AQIQA AND THE CROCUS

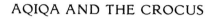

"HAVE you ever looked carefully inside a crocus?" Mrs Burns asked her class.

She took several pots of golden yellow crocuses and the children passed them around. They all had a good look.

"Inside the petals are orange stamens which stand like soldiers around a delicate feathery stigma. The stigmas contain a yellow substance called saffron. It is used to colour and flavour food, especially in Eastern countries like India and Pakistan. Does your mummy use saffron in her cooking, Soraya?"

"Yes," said Soraya. "She puts it in biryani. That's what she makes if special guests are coming. It is meat cooked with rice and yoghurt. The saffron makes the rice turn yellow. She doesn't use it every day, though, because she says it is very expensive. When I was a baby I had saffron put on my head."

"What was that for?" asked Mrs Burns.

"I had my head shaved," said Soraya. "Lots of Muslim babies have their heads shaved just after they are born. They always put saffron water on the head after it has been shaved. It cools the head down."

"I suppose the saffron acts rather like an antiseptic and stops germs getting into any scratches that may happen during shaving," said Mrs Burns. "Who does the shaving, Soraya?"

"When I had my head shaved, my uncle was staying with us and he shaved my head. He is a doctor. He bought me an enormous dolly and I've still got her. When my brother, Imran, and my sister, Hassina, had their heads shaved, a Muslim barber came to our house. He cut their hair with scissors, then shaved their heads with a razor," said Soraya.

Aqiqa and the Crocus

"I remember when Hassina had her hair shaved off," said Sam. "When it started to grow again it stuck up and she looked like a hedgehog."

"Well you'd look like a hedgehog if you had just had your head shaved! " said Soraya indignantly. "Anyway it didn't take long to grow again."

"Why do you do it?" asked Sam.

"It stops you from getting infections and it makes your hair grown strong and healthy," said Soraya. "And you get blessings from God and protection from evil."

"But I didn't get any infections in my head and my brother didn't either and we didn't have our heads shaved," said Sam.

"It is rather confusing for you, Sam; let me try to explain," said Mrs Burns.

"If you look at a tiny baby's head you may notice that the skin on the head looks rather dry and flaky. The mothers wash their babies' heads regularly and sometimes put cream or oil on.

Eventually the dry, flaky skin comes off and leaves a nice clean pink scalp. Some babies do get infections of the scalp even with today's high standard of hygiene. In the days when this tradition started, in a place which is much hotter than we can imagine, there were very poor washing and toilet facilities. This, plus the heat, made infections very common. By shaving the heads of babies the chance of infection was lessened."

"What do you call the head shaving in your language, Soraya?"

"We call it Aqiqa. If you can afford it, you have to sacrifice one goat or lamb if the baby is a girl or two if the baby is a boy. It's like giving something to God because he has been so kind to give a baby to the parents," said Soraya.

"That is interesting, Soraya," said Mrs Burns. "In fact in our own Christian religion we give things because God gave us something. Does anyone know what I'm thinking of?"

"Is it pancakes?" said Peter.

Aqiqa and the Crocus

Aqiqa and the Crocus

"No," said Mrs Burns, with a smile.

"Is it Christmas presents?" said Michael.

"Yes," said Mrs Burns, "but instead of giving them to God we give to our family and friends. What did God give to us at Christmas time?"

"Baby Jesus," said Sarah.

"Yes, quite right," said Mrs Burns.

"What happens to the hair you shave off, Soraya? Do you throw it away?"

"No," said Soraya. "It has to be weighed, and then you give the same weight of silver to the poor people. I have still got my hair, but some people throw it into water or bury it."

"How can you give silver to the poor?" asked Sarah.

"What if you don't have any silver?"

"You can find out the price of silver from the

newspaper and give money instead," said Soraya.

"I think the head shaving has certainly made Soraya's hair grow strong and healthy," said Mrs Burns.

All the class turned to look at Soraya's hair. It was tied in two long silken plaits which went down to her waist.

"It might have grown like that even if it hadn't been shaved," said Sarah. She loved Soraya's hair. Sometimes when they went to parties together, Soraya would wear her hair loose or tied with golden ribbons.

"That is something we can never be certain of," said Mrs Burns, "because she has already had it shaved."

"Do you remember," she went on, "we were talking about the saffron crocus. The names of flowers have meanings. For instance, the apple flower is a symbol of temptation. That goes back to the Old Testament story of Adam and Eve in the Garden of Eden, when Eve tried to tempt

Adam with an apple. The saffron crocus is a symbol of joy, so it seems quite appropriate that a small baby's head is cleansed with it.

"I suppose, instead of writing a letter, you could send a message with flowers. The only problem would be if the person receiving the flowers didn't know their meanings. It would be like trying to read without knowing your letters."

"That's impossible! " said Michael.

"Exactly! " said Mrs Burns.

THE CAR CRASH

MRS Bukhari and her two children were speeding along the M1 motorway towards Birmingham. It was about ten o'clock on a Saturday morning. They made this journey from London every two weeks to visit Mrs Bukhari's family. Usually Mr Bukhari went too, but this particular weekend he had promised to help a friend move house.

The children, Tepoo and Farida, were dozing in the back of the car.

Suddenly there was a terrible thudding noise. The car went out of control and banged into another car on the left. After that the air was filled with the noise of screeching brakes, shattering glass and crunching metal as cars on all sides bumped into each other.

The Car Crash

After a while the noise stopped. People started getting out of their cars. Tepoo and Farida were looking around. Tepoo noticed quite a few cross faces. There were some people crying. Farida looked at her mother. Her face was set calm - but it looked somehow tight. She turned to them and said, "We've had a crash, but thank God we are not hurt, so don't worry. You stay in the car; I'll find out what to do next."

Mrs Bukhari got out. She noticed that her front tyre had blown out. The left side of the car was slightly dented and scratched. But it wasn't too bad. She thought that if she could get the wheel changed, at least she would still be able to drive it.

The police arrived, sirens blaring and lights flashing. They directed the cars on to the hard shoulder so that they could get the traffic moving again. Some of the cars had to be pushed.

Two ambulances arrived, although miraculously no one was hurt. The damage was all to the cars. What a sorry sight some of them looked! A brand new Allegro battered back and front. It could only have been two or three weeks old. A smart little TR7 with a crumpled wing. Mrs Bukhari hardly dared to look. But Tepoo and Farida did. They were busy counting and recounting the number of cars involved. After many differences of opinion they finally agreed on the number seventeen.

Mrs Bukhari felt sick. She had to face the owners of the other sixteen cars, knowing that she was the cause of all this mess. If her tyre hadn't blown out none of this would have happened.

But there was no point thinking like that, so she politely exchanged her name, address and other details with the sixteen other drivers. It seemed never-ending. She gave the children some sweets for being brave. They seemed quite happy to watch all the activity going on around them.

The police had kindly called the AA for Mrs Bukhari and they quickly changed the wheel. She turned the ignition key nervously and prayed. It started, and they were off on the motorway again. They kept in the inside lane and went very slowly.

After twenty miles they saw a sign for the

The Car Crash

Services. It was well past their usual lunchtime and the children were hungry, so they went into the cafe.

They ate cheese sandwiches and cream cakes and drank Coca Cola. Mrs Bukhari drank three cups of coffee.

There was only forty-five minutes' journey left and it passed without a hitch.

Farida and Tepoo charged in to see their grandmother. Their mother followed behind, relieved to have arrived. She could hear the children chattering in Urdu. Her mouth gaped open in surprise when she heard them. They were saying, "Oh, you should have been with us Grandma. It was the best journey ever. We had a crash and saw lots of break-down wagons and police cars and ambulances, and we talked to a policeman, and Mummy gave us sweets for being brave and we had our lunch in a cafe."

At that moment Mrs Bukhari entered the room and greeted her mother. "Assalamu alaikum," she said, meaning - peace be with you. It was the traditional Muslim greeting.

Her mother replied, "Wa alaikumus salam" - and peace be with you too! "

These were always the first words they said to each other - but today they seemed to mean something extra.

SHEREEN IS THOUGHTFUL

IT was ten to twelve on a Monday morning and Sam was looking at the clock. He had finished his piece of work. In fact it was the fourth piece of work he had done that morning and he was feeling very pleased with himself.

His tummy started rumbling. " I'm starving! " he whispered to Antonio, who was sitting next to him.

"So am I," said Antonio. "I'm so hungry, I could eat a hundred chips."

Shereen was listening into this conversation - she had finished her work too. She was very hungry, and normally she would have joined in the conversation and said that she could have eaten two hundred chips or even twenty hundred chips -

23

but she was thinking. She was thinking of her
mother and father.

Shereen's family were Muslims and it was the
month of Ramazan. Every year during the month
of Ramazan Shereen's parents fasted. They could
not eat or drink even a drop of water from dawn
until sunset. This particular year Ramazan had
come in July. Because the Muslim year is eleven
days shorter than the Christian year, the Muslim
and Christian months are always out of line with
each other. In England the July days are very long
and on this particular day Shereen's parents would
be fasting from 2.55 a.m. until 9.30 p.m. That
meant no food or water for eighteen hours and
thirty-five minutes.

"My mum and dad are fasting," said Shereen
thoughtfully. "They can't eat anything all day."

"That's easy-peasy," said Sam. "I bet I could fast
for a whole week."

"You couldn't," said Shereen. "Look at you - you
could hardly wait for your dinner."

Shereen is Thoughtful

"Anyway, you'd die," piped in Daniel, who'd heard Sam boasting about fasting for a whole week.

"What is all this chatter about?" called Mrs Burns in a sharp voice. "Have you all finished your work?"

"Yes, Mrs Burns," they all chanted, although Daniel and Antonio had not really.

"Put away your books then," said Mrs Burns.

When they had tidied up their tables, the children went to the cloakroom to wash ready for dinner. They forgot about fasting. Dinner was tasty - meat pie, chips and carrots, with jelly and biscuits to follow.

At playtime they played their favourite game, 'Boys against the Girls'. A boy would catch a girl and then the other girls would try to free her. Sometimes the girls would try to kiss the boys to make them run away from where they were keeping guard. You see they hated being kissed more than anything.

Shereen is Thoughtful

Mrs France, the dinner lady, clapped her hands for 'in-time'. When everyone had sat down at their tables, Mrs Burns pointed to the table where Sam, Antonio, Shereen and Daniel were sitting.

"Now you four," she said, "what were you talking about before dinner?" Mrs Burns had been listening in to what they had been saying. She turned to Shereen.

"Didn't you say that your mummy and daddy were fasting?"

"Yes," said Shereen, "because it's Ramazan."

"Can any of the class remember when the Christian people fast?" asked Mrs Burns.

"Is it on Pancake Day?" asked Peter.

"Well, you are very near," said Mrs Burns. "Pancake Day is the day before the Christian people start their fast. They use all the things in their cupboards like flour, eggs, milk and other left-overs and they make them into pancakes, then they are ready to fast. You could say it's a feast before a fast.

Shereen is Thoughtful

Pancake Day is also called Shrove Tuesday. "Shrove" comes from an old word - "shrive" which means "to confess". It was the custom to confess, that is to tell God all your wrong doings before fasting."

"Did any of you have pancakes on Shrove Tuesday?"

"Yes! " called a lot of the children.

"I had jam on mine," said Sam.

"I had lemon and sugar on mine," said Daniel.

"I had sausage and beans on mine," said Toby.

"What comes after Shrove Tuesday?" asked Mrs Burns.

"Ash Wednesday! " called out John.

"That's right," said Mrs Burns, "and Ash Wednesday is the first day of Lent. The word "Lent" comes from another old word - "lencten" which means "lengthen". During the forty days and forty nights of fasting, the days lengthen as they approach Easter. So that is how the forty days and forty nights of fasting became known as Lent. It is a time when the Christian people remember Jesus being tempted by the devil in the wilderness, during his fast.

"Have any of you children ever given anything up for Lent?" asked Mrs Burns.

The children shook their heads.

"We don't have to, do we?" asked Sam.

"No," said Mrs Burns, "you don't have to; it is up to each person whether they fast and what things they choose to give up. When I was young I often used to give up chocolate. Then at Easter, when Lent was over, my parents would buy me an Easter egg. It used to taste twice as delicious after not having had any chocolate for nearly six weeks.

"If you are a Muslim you have to fast," said Shereen. She could not quite understand why things seemed so free and easy in the Christian faith. "My brother is ten and he kept his first fast on Saturday. We had a great big party to celebrate and all our relatives and friends came round. My parents are teaching him to fast so that he'll be able to do it all when he's older. I'm not old enough to keep a fast yet."

"How long do your parents have to fast for, Shereen?" asked Mrs Burns.

"It's for a month," said Shereen, "until they see the new moon of Shawwal."

"What is Shawwal?" asked Daniel.

"It's the name of the month that comes after Ramazan," said Shereen.

"Aren't they funny words!" said Sam, giggling.

"Well, not really," said Mrs Burns. "It is just because you aren't used to hearing them."

"If you don't eat and drink for a month, you will die," said Daniel, absolutely convinced he was right.

29

Shereen is Thoughtful

"But you can eat and drink when it's dark," said Shereen. She thought everyone knew these things.

"If I was a Muslim I'd eat all night and sleep all day," said Daniel.

"No, no! " said Shereen. She was feeling a bit worried. Nobody ever joked about Ramazan at home. It was something serious.

"You have to carry on with all the ordinary things, but you have to be extra kind and try to do things for people and think about the poor people and always be thinking about God."

"I should think that if you did all that, you would be a much nicer person to know," said Mrs Burns. "Perhaps that is what fasting teaches us - after all, people have been fasting since the days of the Old Testament. That is, for thousands of years. It must be good for us. Not only the Christians and Muslims fast, but also the Hindus, the Jews and many others.

"Now Shereen, as you have told us so much about your way of fasting, and helped us to understand it, perhaps you would like to choose a book for the story."

Shereen smiled. She suddenly felt rather special. She went to the shelf and chose her favourite story, "Horton Hatches the Egg", which was all about an elephant who hatched an egg containing an "elephant bird". Who ever heard of such a thing!

THE TOILE-T-ISSUE

NINA was playing at Shereen's house for the morning. It was raining so they decided to do some colouring. After some time Shereen's mummy brought them a drink and a biscuit.

"What shall we play next?" asked Shereen, when she had finished her drink.

"Just a minute," said Nina, "I want to go to the toilet." She rushed off to the downstairs bathroom. Oops! No toilet paper! Only a strange looking silver pot on the floor. She needed paper so she rushed to the upstairs bathroom. No paper! Just the same strange silver pot on the floor.

What was she to do? Well, she would just have to manage without paper. She left the bathroom, feeling uncomfortable, and went downstairs to find Shereen.

The Toile-t-issue

"Don't you have toilet paper at your house?" asked Nina.

"Yes, we do usually, in case anyone comes," said Shereen, "but we don't use it ourselves."

"What do you do then?" asked Nina, amazed.

"We use the lota," said Shereen.

"What is the lota?" asked Nina.

Shereen was surprised that Nina didn't know all these things. "The lota is the silver pot we keep in the bathroom. We fill it with warm water, pour it with our right hand, and wash ourselves with our left hand," she said.

"Why do you wash with your left hand?" asked Nina, thinking that it was always easier to do things with your right hand - if you're right-handed, that is.

"Because we use our right hand for eating," said Shereen.

"I thought you ate with a knife and fork," said Nina. "I've seen you at school."

"Well I do at school," said Shereen, "but at home I eat with my right hand."

"When I saw those silver pots, I thought they were a kind of watering can for plants," said Nina.

"That's a good idea," said Shereen. So they both filled up a lota and went all round the house watering the pot plants.

IMRAN'S BISMILLAH

IN Sam's class, there was a little Indian girl called Soraya. Sam had known her ever since playgroup. He also knew her brother Imran and her sister Hassina - but they weren't old enough to go to school yet. Although Sam's friends were mainly boys, he did like Soraya. She had been to one of his parties and Sam remembered her beautiful, glittering Indian dress.

Sam was eating his breakfast. It was a school day which meant he had to eat quickly. There never seemed to be much time on school mornings. His mummy came into the room waving an invitation.

"Look Sam, Soraya's mummy and daddy have invited all our family to go to Imran's Bismillah ceremony."

Imran's Bismillah

"What is a Bismillah ceremony?" said Sam.

"I don't know," said his mummy - "but it sounds exciting. We'll have to find out when we go."

"Let's ask Soraya what Imran would like for a present when we get to school."

Sam was so excited on the way to school. He wanted to know what Imran had to do, and whether Soraya would wear Indian clothes and whether his mummy was going to wear a sari like Soraya's mummy did.

"Calm down, Sam!" said his mummy. "The party isn't until next week, so we've got plenty of time to find out everything."

The following Sunday afternoon at two o'clock, Sam's family were ready to leave the house. His daddy wore a suit and his mummy her best dress. Sam and his brother Ben were wearing new trousers. Sam was carrying the present. Soraya had said that Imran was very keen on painting, so they had bought him some face paints, finger paints and a big roll of thick paper. Ben, who was a bit older than Sam, had made a card with Bismillah on it because they couldn't find one in the shops.

When they arrived at the Hall they saw lots of other people driving up in their cars. Whole families piled out, some with two children, some with three - in one car Sam counted six children. There were Indian and English people. Soraya, Imran, Hassina and their parents were waiting to greet their guests. They all looked so smart. Imran had a blue kurta, which is a loose shirt, and matching trousers called pyjamas. Then he wore a blue and gold waistcoat and a golden hat. His daddy wore a gold coat called a sherwani and the slippers on his feet curled up into a circle at the toes. His mummy wore a blue and golden sari and lots of jewellery. Soraya and Hassina had blue kurta pyjama sets with golden lace and sequins sewn on.

By three o'clock all the guests had arrived. Everybody sat on chairs in front of the stage and Imran was led by his parents to a specially prepared bed covered with a large cloth. He sat down and his mother put flowers on him and fitted on a special head dress called serah, which had long glittering threads that hung down each side of his face.

His grandfather came on to the stage and he said some words from the Koran (which is the holy book of the Muslim people). He said them very loudly and slowly so that Imran could repeat them.

Afterwards, Imran's grandmother came on to the stage with a plate of golden yellow sweets called ladoos. They looked rather like golden golf balls. She offered them to Imran and he took one. Then Imran's grandfather explained the Arabic words which Imran had repeated. They were the first words that God had revealed to Mohammed the Prophet of the Muslim religion.

The general message was that a person should learn to read and write and gain as much knowledge as possible, but that the knowledge itself comes from God.

There was more talking and some poetry recital, then the ceremony was over.

Imran's Bismillah

On came the Indian dancers. Sam had never seen anything like it. The music was strange, the clothes colourful. The way the ladies moved their hands and heads was almost magical. Sam tried but couldn't make his fingers do what he wanted them to do.

When the dancing was over the chairs were moved away and the guests chatted while the children played.

Sam tried to find Soraya among the crowd of guests. At last he found her.

"It's funny seeing you here instead of in school," said Sam.

"Do you like this Bismillah party?" said Soraya.

"Yes, " said Sam, "but why do you have to have one?"

"Imran is four years, four months and four days old, so he has his Bismillah. I had mine when I was four years, four months and four days old," said Soraya.

Imran's Bismillah

"Yes, but why do you do it anyway?"

"Well, you are supposed to be old enough to start learning to read at that age, so it's like your first lesson," said Soraya.

"It's a funny way to start learning to read. Why don't you have flash cards like we do at school?" said Sam, feeling puzzled.

"Well, we are Muslims and our holy book, the Koran, is a very special book, so it is a good book to start on," said Soraya.

"Why don't we start by reading the Bible instead of flash cards?" asked Sam, still unconvinced.

"I don't know," said Soraya, "but the Lord's Prayer is in the Bible and we have learnt that off by heart. So we do learn from the Bible and from flash cards at school."

At last Sam seemed satisfied.

Something was happening; everyone had gone

Imran's Bismillah

quiet and a loud voice was calling the guests to come and enjoy the food.

On one long table there were plates piled high with saffron coloured rice, tureens of steaming curries, bowls of chutneys, trays of kebabs, poppadums (which are like huge round crisps). On another table were the sweets, tropical fruit salad with lychees, mangoes and guavas, chilled keer which is like rice pudding but nicer, green, yellow, white and orange milk sweets in different shapes and sizes.

"It smells as though we are in a different country," said Sam, his eyes wide. "Do I like any of these things, mummy?"

"I don't know," said his mummy. "You can try whatever you like, but come and look at your own table first."

Sam hadn't realised that he had been looking at the grown-up food. He sat down with the rest of the children and tucked into sandwiches, crisps, cheese, cakes, biscuits and ice-cream and fizzy pop to drink.

Imran's Bismillah

Later on, when his mummy came over to check whether he was all right, Sam pinched a kebab off her plate and was quite surprised to find how tasty it was.

Sam noticed that some of the grown-ups were eating the food with their fingers. Somehow they managed to do it without getting the rest of their hand dirty. He thought they were very clever to do that.

Imran was having a wonderful time. He had finished his food and was inspecting the table where all his presents had been kept. Sam went over to see Imran.

"You've got even more presents that we get at Christmas. Do you have Christmas presents as well?"

"Oh yes," said Imran. "I'm double lucky! "

"It's time for us to go now, Sam," said his mummy. "Imran will be going soon and when he goes home he will have all those presents to open."

"I have eaten so much lovely food that I'm sure I won't be able to eat another thing until tomorrow."

"Was it like the food you get from the Indian Takeaway every Friday?" asked Sam.

"Oh, it was much, much better than that," said his mummy. "Come along, we'll say our thankyous and goodbyes."

THE BEST PLACE ON EARTH

ONE afternoon Mrs Burns was talking to her class. She asked them the question - "Can you tell me one word which means the best place on earth?" On the blackboard was written the word UTOPIA. Mrs Burns said that was her word for the best place on earth.

The children called out some other suggestions and Mrs Burns wrote these down too.

There was Wonderland; Dreamland; the Garden of Eden; Paradise and Mecca.

"Now children," said Mrs Burns, "I would like you to copy all these words down in your work books, then choose one and write about it."

Shereen decided to write about Mecca as it had

been her suggestion. She knew quite a lot about it because it was always being mentioned at home. Her grandparents had been there. Also, when she went to her weekly classes to learn about her religion, Islam, she had learnt about Mecca.

She wrote this:

"Mecca is a city in a very hot country called Saudi Arabia. Saudi Arabia is mostly desert. Every year in the season of pilgrimage Muslims from all over the world go to Mecca. Every Muslim has to go for pilgrimage once in his life if he has enough money. The holy prophet Mohammed (peace be upon him) was born in Mecca. There is a holy mosque there and inside it is the kaaba which is the house of God. It is covered with a big cloth. If you go there you are nearer to God than anywhere else in the world."

After about half an hour everyone had finished so Mrs Burns called Sam to the front of the class and asked him to read what he had put.

Sam read - "Paradise - Paradise is where all your friends are. It is sunny during the day and rains at night. You don't have to go to school but there are lots of interesting things to do. In Paradise the roads are big and wide and every boy is given a free sports car to drive around in."

Some of the girls groaned a bit when he said this.

"What's the matter, Holly?" asked Mrs Burns.

"Well, it isn't fair that only boys are allowed to ride the sports cars," said Holly.

"This is just Sam's idea of Paradise," said Mrs Burns. "Perhaps your idea would be different. What did you write about, Holly?"

Holly had written about Wonderland. According to her, Wonderland was full of wonderful things like houses made of sweets, taps from which came coca cola and lemonade, trees decorated with jewels and fairy lights. The class listened eagerly as Holly read aloud.

Mrs Burns said that one person could read for each of the words on the blackboard. But nobody had chosen Utopia, so Mrs Burns explained that it

The Best Place on Earth

was an imaginary place where everything was perfect.

Only Michael had written about the Garden of Eden. He had learnt about it at Sunday School the week before and it had stuck in his mind. His Sunday School teacher had described it as a garden planted by God which contained beautiful, colourful flowers and plants which could be eaten. It was watered by a river and there were creatures of every kind. They had all helped to make a picture of how they imagined the Garden of Eden to be and it had worked out very well. The grown ups all came to admire it.

Most of the children had written about Dreamland. Of course in dreams anything can happen. Toby was chosen to read his. Daniel suggested that because it was about Dreamland he ought to read it with his eyes closed. So Toby closed his eyes - and then he realised he couldn't see so he peeped out of one eye. Even Mrs Burns couldn't help laughing.

Two children had written about Mecca, Shereen and Soraya. Surprisingly they both had written almost the same thing.

"Why do you think Soraya and Shereen have written nearly the same thing?" Mrs Burns asked the class.

"Because they copied," said Sam.

"That's impossible," said Mrs Burns. "They don't even sit at the same table."

"Because they have the same religion," said Michael.

"You and Holly have the same religion, Michael, but you had different ideas for the best place on earth," said Mrs Burns, "but you are partly right. They are both Muslims and in their religion they are taught that Mecca is the best place on earth to be. But why did they write almost the same things about Mecca? A lot of you wrote about Dreamland but all your stories were different."

"Because Mecca is a real place and they know what it's like," said Sarah.

"Yes," said Mrs Burns. "All the other places on the blackboard like Utopia, Wonderland, Dreamland

and Paradise are all in your imagination. That is why you can make them into whatever you want them to be."

"And the Garden of Eden," said Michael, thinking that he had been left out.

"I did leave that one out on purpose, Michael," said Mrs Burns, "because it isn't really in your imagination. It is a place mentioned in the Bible at the beginning of the world, before there was any wickedness. A place where there is no wickedness must surely be one of the best places on earth. The problem is, all this happened so long ago nobody is sure where the Garden of Eden was."

Later that day Shereen asked her mother if Mecca was the best place on earth.

"Yes, of course it is," said her mother. "Why do you ask?"

"We all wrote about what we thought was the best place on earth at school today. I wrote about Mecca and so did Soraya, but everyone else's stories seemed to be much more fun. Do Muslims have fun when they go to Mecca on pilgrimage?" asked Shereen.

"No," said her mother. "You don't go on your pilgrimage for fun. It is something you do just for the sake of God and if you do it properly God forgives you for all the wrong things you have done. It gives you a great feeling of happiness and peace which lasts longer than a bit of fun."

"I remember last year, when your grandfather came back from performing his pilgrimage, some people asked him, "Did you have a good time?" as if he had been on a holiday. Of course he didn't mind - he just told everybody that it was more than a good time; it was the most important and special thing he had done in his life."

"Do Christian people go for pilgrimage?" asked Shereen.

"Yes, some of them do go to visit the holy places like Bethlehem, Jerusalem, the Sea of Galilee - in fact all the places which Jesus (peace be upon him) travelled to while taking his message to the people.

The Best Place on Earth

"The difference is, Shereen, that Christian people do not have to perform pilgrimage. They can choose whether they want to do it or not, whereas in Islam we have to do it and we want to do it. It is part of our faith."

"Isn't it a good thing to have a choice?" asked Shereen.

"It is very nice to have a choice," said her mother, "but it does have its dangers. People can be very lazy about doing things when they have a choice. If you had the choice of going to school or not, you may choose not to go. As a result, you wouldn't learn anything. If you had the choice of saying your prayers or not, you may choose not to say them. As a result you would never talk to God."

"If I had the choice between eating my dinner and not eating it, then I would eat it," said Shereen.

"Then you've made the right choice," said her mother smiling. "I've made parathas and kebabs."

"Lovely! " said Shereen, and she followed her mother into the kitchen to help set the table.

SHAMA GOES TO A FANCY-DRESS PARTY

SHAMA was beside herself with excitement, because today was the day of the party. This party was even more special than usual because it was the party of her best friend, Kathy, and it was also a fancy-dress party.

It was time for Shama to get dressed. She was going to dress up as a Red Indian squaw. Her dress was made from one of her mummy's old kaftans. Underneath she wore long, thick, orange socks - they were her winter socks that she wore with her wellies. On her feet she wore moccasin slippers. Around her waist she wore a bead belt which her mummy had worn when she was a teenager in the days of "Flower Power". The large feather on her headband had been found on a visit to a wild life park. She had learnt how to made a papoose at school. To go inside it she had selected one of her dark-haired dollies and had made a tiny head dress for her.

Shama's long hair was tied in two, thick plaits - even though her mother was English, Shama's skin was almost as dark as her father's. He was an Indian. With her lovely brown skin and the outfit, she made a perfect Red Indian squaw.

When she arrived at Kathy's party she was very interested to see what the others were wearing. There was a red pillar box, a black crow, a ladybird, a white rabbit, a fairy, batman, a surgeon, Worzel Gummidge, a clown, a cowboy, a punk and a bride.

When all the children had arrived, Kathy's mummy made everyone stand in a circle. She put a wooden box in the middle and called each child on to the box to answer a few questions.

When it was Shama's turn, she said, "Come along, Shama, and stand on the box. Now, who are you dressed up as?"

"I'm a Red Indian squaw," said Shama.

Shama Goes to a Party

"And is that your baby on your back?" asked Kathy's mummy.

Shama nodded.

"How old is she?"

"She isn't even one," said Shama.

"Are you a real Red Indian?" asked Kathy's mummy, "because you look just like one."

Shama smiled shyly, because she knew Kathy's mummy was teasing a bit.

"I am half Indian," said Shama, "but it's a different sort of Indian."

"That's right, you're an Asian Indian. I have got a lollipop here for you," said Kathy's mummy, handing Shama the lollipop, "for speaking so nicely and looking so beautiful."

Shama said thank you, everyone clapped and she got down and went to stand in the circle. All the children had a lollipop after they had spoken.

Shama Goes to a Party

"I think you are all terrific," said Kathy's mummy. "I have given the difficult job of choosing three winners to Kathy's daddy."

Kathy's daddy came and stood on the box. "The third prize goes to the pillar box," said Kathy's daddy. Everyone clapped and the pillar box shuffled into the middle to receive his prize.

"The second prize goes to the Red Indian squaw," said Kathy's daddy. The fairy who was sitting next to Shama gave her a nudge. But Shama was already on her feet, going to receive her prize. Second prize! How wonderful! What could it be? She tried to make her face serious when she looked at Kathy's daddy. He gave her a little pink notebook and said, "Well done." When she got back to her place she was beaming with delight. The fairy was still clapping enthusiastically for her. She couldn't wait to see what Shama had won.

"Last, but not least, the first prize of the fancy-dress competition goes to the ladybird," said Kathy's daddy. One very happy ladybird with feelers flapping went to receive his prize. He got a notebook and a pencil with a rubber on top.

Shama Goes to a Party

There were lots of games to follow, then a special tea. Every child had their own box covered in bright paper. The inside was filled with nice things to eat: a bottle of pop and a little surprise present. As it was a lovely sunny day they all took their boxes outside into the garden.

After tea all the mums arrived to collect their children. Shama thought it had been the best party ever.

THE CLASS PERFORM WAZU

IT was a normal sort of Tuesday morning. The children were playing around outside. When it was time to go in, they filed into their classrooms as usual. But what a surprise for Class Three! It was their teacher, Mrs Burns. At least, they thought it was her. She was looking quite different - in a nice sort of way. She had a completely different hair style - it had been long and straight, but now it was short and curly. Also, she was wearing some very smart clothes which the children hadn't seen before.

Mrs Burns grinned at all their enquiring faces. "I'm sure you're all dying to know why I am looking like this," she said. "The reason is, that straight after school, I am driving to London Airport to meet my brother who I haven't seen for five years. He has been living in New Zealand, which is on the other side of the world. I wanted to look my best.

"Do you think I look better than before?" she asked. There was a chorus of children saying yes and no, in which the yes's were slightly louder than the no's.

"What would you all do if you were meeting someone special?" asked Mrs Burns.

"I'd go to bed early the night before," said Daniel.

"You'd never sleep," said Toby. "I never do when I go to bed early."

"I'd buy him a present," said Michael.

"What would you do if you were going to meet God?" asked Mrs Burns.

"I'd have a bath and wash my hair," said Peter.

"I would wear my best clothes," said Sarah.

"What do you think you would say to God?" asked Mrs Burns.

The Class Perform Wazu

"I'd wait and see what he said to me first," said Sam thoughtfully, "and then try to be very polite when I answered him."

"I'd say something nice to him, like thank you for all the good things in the world," said Shereen.

"We don't call him God, we call him Allah," said Soraya.

"Yes," said Mrs Burns, "Muslim people call God Allah, but the words have the same meaning. It is just a difference in language. What would you do, Soraya, if you were meeting Allah?"

"I would do what we do for prayers," said Soraya, without hesitation.

When Soraya was four years, four months and four days old, she had celebrated her Bismillah - which was like her first lesson towards becoming a Muslim. Since then she had been learning about the Muslim religion. She was now seven.

"What do you do for prayers?" asked Mrs Burns.

The Class Perform Wazu

"First we do wazu," said Soraya.

"Wazu sounds like the zoo," said Peter, giggling, which as usual set Antonio off as well.

"That's enough, boys! " said Mrs Burns. "What is wazu, Soraya?" Actually, she had thought it sounded like the zoo as well.

"Wazu is a special way of washing yourself," said Soraya.

"Yes, I do that too," said Shereen, who was also a Muslim.

"I've got an idea," said Mrs Burns. "Why don't you two come to the front and pretend you are doing wazu. All the rest of the class will copy what you do."

Soraya and Shereen walked out to the front. They were good friends. They didn't mind showing the others how to do wazu.

First they washed their hands and in between their fingers three times. Then they washed their

The Class Perform Wazu

mouths and teeth three times. They seemed to be doing everything at exactly the same time without even looking at each other. It was obviously something they were used to doing. Next they washed and blew their noses three times, which caused great hilarity, resulting in half a dozen of the class having to rush to the toilet to wipe their noses on some toilet paper.

After the interruption they continued by washing their faces three times. The whole class was absorbed in copying every move Shereen and Soraya made. They even copied Shereen when she scratched her nose, which wasn't part of the wazu at all.

They washed their right hands and arms up to their elbows three times, and repeated the same on the left. Then they wiped their hair three times, cleaned their ears inside and out three times, and finally washed their right foot and ankle and then left foot and ankle three times.

"That is a lot of washing," said Mrs Burns. "You have to do that every time before you pray, don't you?"

The Class Perform Wazu

"Yes," said Shereen, "and if you are a true Muslim you pray five times a day."

There were gasps of amazement from the class at the thought of having to wash so many times in one day.

"After you have performed wazu, are you ready to pray?" asked Mrs Burns.

"It has to be the right time," said Soraya, "and you have to be wearing the right sort of clothes. Girls and women have to cover all of their bodies and their heads, boys and men have to cover from their waist to their knees and have something on their heads."

"You have to put your prayer mat on the floor," said Shereen, "and it has to face Mecca."

"I think you are right, Soraya, to think that you would prepare for meeting God in the same way that you prepare for praying to God, After all, praying is the time when you talk to God."

"We don't have to wash before we pray," said Sam.

"It is just different people's ways of staying close to God," said Mrs Burns. "I am sure that those of you who go to church or Sunday School have a good wash and wear clean clothes before you leave your houses."

"Well, this morning you have all performed wazu before your assembly prayers - even though you didn't use water. Can you lead in quietly? We have been so busy chatting, I haven't even called the register. We must do it after assembly."

SEMINA'S MISTAKE

MRS Chadda looked at her watch. She just had time to go down to the Asian grocer's before she picked up her daughter, Semina, from school.

She bought mangoes, oranges and some carra - which is a sort of spicy mixture of dry nuts, corn, lentils and things like that. Mr Chadda loved it, but Semina thought it was too spicy.

She took the shopping home, washed the fruit and put it into a dish, and emptied the carra into a powdered milk tin to keep it fresh. Normally she would have gone straight to school with her shopping but today was an unusual day. It was the day that Humphrey the school hamster was coming to their house. Mrs Chadda would have to have her hands free to carry the cage.

Semina's Mistake

Semina came dashing to the school gate, bright-eyed with excitement, while her teacher followed slowly behind, balancing a three-tier hamster cage on one arm and a cardboard box on the other.

Semina agreed to carry the cardboard box, while her mummy carried the cage. "I hope Humphrey will like it with us," said Semina.

"I'm sure he won't mind where he is, as long as he is fed and kept clean," said mummy.

"Can I feed him when we get home?" asked Semina.

"OK," said mummy.

It was only a few minutes' walk from the school to their home. Mrs Chadda's sister was at home looking after Yusuf and Yasmin, Semina's brother and sister.

Yusuf and Yasmin were pleased to see Semina, but they were even more pleased to see Humphrey.

Semina's Mistake

"Semina, could you unpack the box on to the kitchen table, while I find a quiet place for Humphrey?" asked mummy.

"Yes, I'll do it," said Semina, feeling important. She took out a bag of sawdust, a packet of woolly bedding material, a list of instructions and a tin of food. Then she rushed around looking for her mummy. At last she found her in the garden shed. "Can I feed Humphrey now?" asked Semina.

"Yes, of course," said mummy.

When Semina went back to the kitchen table she noticed two tins which looked exactly alike. She only remembered unpacking one - but perhaps mummy had already unpacked one. She opened both tins and looked inside. They looked similar - so she took one tin and filled Humphrey's dish from it.

Yusuf and Yasmin came to watch Humphrey feed. First he sniffed around and then he began to stuff his pouches. His face became fatter and fatter. Then he began to move around rather quickly. He kept touching his nose and his mouth with his front paws as if something was itching. He went up to his sleeping quarters, quickly emptied his pouches and came down again. He had a drink then touched his nose and mouth with his paws again; then he had another drink.

"Mummy!" shouted Semina. "I think Humphrey is drinking too much."

Mummy came to look.

"No wonder he's drinking," said mummy. "You've given him daddy's carra."

"Poor Humphrey! Do you think he'll die?" asked Semina, remembering how she had felt once when she had eaten some very spicy carra.

"I'm sure he'll be OK," said mummy. "I don't suppose he actually swallowed any of it. He just put it into his pouches. We'll clean out his bedding and give him some fresh food."

Later in the afternoon, Mr Chadda came home from work. The children were playing in the garden and Mrs Chadda and her sister were chatting and watching the children. Mr Chadda went into the kitchen looking for someone to say hello to. He saw the carra tin on the table and decided to have a nibble. He went into the garden, putting a handful into his mouth. When Mrs Chadda saw him he had a strange expression on his face and was chewing something with difficulty.

"What's the matter, Yaseen?" she asked.

"It's this carra," he said.

At this point Mrs Chadda burst out laughing.

"It's not carra, Yaseen, it's hamster food."

He spat the hamster food out in digust. "But we haven't even got a hamster! " he said in exasperation.

Semina thought it was hilarious that her daddy had made the same mistake as she had.

That evening after they had eaten their evening meal, daddy asked the children whether they would like a mango. They all said yes - it was their favourite fruit.

"Can I give some to Humphrey?" asked Semina.

"Yes, if you like," said daddy laughing. "Let's make his stay here a complete Asian experience."

THE END